REBUILDING YOUR MARRIAGE

A Process of Self-Evaluation

By George Bissett

Acknowledgements

Bob Bray and his wife, Dawn, motivated me to write out what I had been yakking about over many meals and coffees. Thanks.

Bob's biography and writings can be found on our website www.dynamicdiscovery.ca

Heartfelt thanks to Christina (Chrissy) Rice who has organized and formatted my words and has been the driving force behind getting this book into a readable format.

Chrissy may be found on her own website, http://completeadminsolutions.ca/

And, I can never forget all the very wise and patient people who are members of the same anonymous groups as me – you know who you are. I hope you know that I love you all.

Table of Contents

Introduction

If it feels like you're missing something in life, maybe it's time to try something different.

This workbook will show you how apply a simple, but life-changing process to accomplish that.

First, here's a starter question: Would you sooner be right or happy?

Both are a choice. You can make a conscious decision to pick one over the other, and we can show you how to do that ... if you can answer the question: Right ___ Happy ___

If you chose 'Right', then there is "sort of" a solution to your problem; "sort of" because it requires that your partner have a codependent personality, which is defined as 'a psychological condition or a relationship in which a person is controlled or manipulated by another who is affected with a pathological condition'. In broader terms, it refers to the dependence on the needs of or control of another. It also often involves placing a lower priority on one's own needs while being excessively preoccupied with the needs of others.

Codependency can occur in any type of relationship including family, work, friendship, and also romantic, peer or community relationships. Codependency may also be characterized by denial, low self-esteem, excessive compliance, or control patterns. Narcissists are considered to be natural magnets for the codependent.

In other words, the codependent partner believes and/or acts as though they only exist to please their partner.

If you chose 'Happy', then there is a definite solution to your problem and we will address that solution as we go along.

For now, you may be reading this because your marriage is dangling from a ledge. You may be here because you're trying to avoid the mistakes of previous relationships. You may be here because you have suffered some level of distress – from obvious symptoms to quiet panic – because things are not the way you had hoped. You may be just looking for more effective ways to communicate with your partner.

Whether your marriage is troubled or you just want more from it, you have probably gone through long periods of soul-searching and self-confession while attempting to learn what one does to become a good partner.

The Starting Point

It is not unusual for us to get a call from someone (usually a woman) who says, "Our marriage is in trouble but (my partner) won't go to counseling with me. What can I do?"

Let's pause to consider the situation ...

When one partner suggests bringing a counselor into their marriage problems, the other partner either hears an alarm while envisioning being attacked by their partner and the counselor, or imagines the stories that their partner and the counselor will release to the world. Confidentiality be damned! Anxiety, panic, and other fear-based emotions fill their mind and affect their mental and physical health – hence the old saying about becoming sick and tired of thinking about unpleasant things. Unpleasant things that may not have happened ... yet.

A fearful person will not want to discuss personal issues (maybe even sexual issues) with a stranger. A fearful person will wonder how a stranger could possibly know enough to fix their marital problems. A fearful person will wonder what a stranger could possibly say that would make a difference. A fearful person will wonder why people who are like them – intelligent, competent people – wouldn't be able to solve their problems on their own.

A fearful person will want their secrets to remain secret. A fearful person will almost always reject help because ... well, after all, weren't we taught that winners never quit and quitters never win? "Yeah ... that's it ... I ain't no stinkin' quitter."

And so on ... and on ... and on ...

The usual result in situations like this is strong resistance, arguments that escalate from somewhat calm to really, really loud. And both partners are left feeling frustrated and hopeless.

Feeling fear can be very unpleasant, but attempting to suppress those emotions is not helpful, so here are a few good questions to ask yourself about fear:

• What exactly am I afraid of?

_____

• Is it really realistic or just a possibility?

_____

• What is the absolute worst that can happen?

_____

_____

• What can I do that I'm not doing now to protect myself from that outcome?

_____

_____

• Where in my body do I feel fear?

_____

• How do I feel when I take a few deep breaths?

_____

Five Suggestions For Dealing With Your Partner

It would be important and informative if your partner would agree to address the suggestions at the same time as you – address, not commit to anything more than that. Surely there's nothing to lose in merely addressing it if there is no additional requirement. For now.

1. Ask for 10 minutes to address the objection(s).

Because the primary problem appears to be stubborn defensiveness, the real problem is fear. Be straight with your partner and ask them – without being demanding – to help you understand. For the fearful person, once the fear is identified, it can be addressed and acknowledged as to why it is real for them. They can then consider accepting that their fear may come true or may not – but is more likely to happen if it is obsessed about.

Then one must determine whether they have done what is within their control to do: If not, then the things not yet done must be listed and acted upon; if there is nothing more to do, then it is time to move on.

You can calm the waters by admitting that you have a big part in resolving your differences, but it takes two people to have a conflict and two people to solve it. It's important for each partner to look at their part and how they can, together, improve their partnership.

2. Describe the benefit to your partner.

Consider what your partner's perspective might be. What would he or she get out of seeking help?

You could suggest that it would make you happy and would show you that he/she is making an effort. You could also suggest that it would help both of you to understand each other better and the two of you will likely learn some new skills/techniques that would decrease your arguing and allow you to have more fun.

3. Pique his or her interest.

Find an article, e-book, podcast, or a video on YouTube – or on our website (www.DynamicDiscovery.ca) and ask your partner to read, watch, or listen. You can use this as a conversation starter. Ask your partner what he or she thought about it or what part he or she related to. Then share your thoughts. Make your partner the expert on the topic and ask if he or she thinks most men/women feel that way.

4. Use the term 'coaching' instead of 'counseling'.

Going for coaching sessions puts the focus on learning new skills and techniques and off the prospect of blame and who is right and who is wrong and whose personality needs to change. Many men, in particular, often can relate to a coaching metaphor, as sports teams need a good coach to be their best, for example.

5. Ask your partner to talk to the coach – alone – just once and test it.

He or she may resist less if it's understood that the commitment is for just one introductory session. It is important that your partner meet the Coach and ask questions he or she may not ask in front of you. After meeting the Coach, he or she may see the value and want to continue. Also, this moves the fear of the unknown out of the way.

6. Deal-makers and deal-breakers

In order to structure the terms of a relationship (the rules by which it's administered), make a list of deal-makers and deal-breakers. Please note that the list is not to be a list of the things you want your partner to do and what you are willing to do to make it possible. The list is to be YOUR deal-makers and/or deal-breakers to enable you to remain in the relationship.

The list is usually three or four (or five or six) points – such as: "I will not accept (insert the issue or behavior here)," or "I must have (insert the issue or behavior here)."

The kicker here is that you MUST be sincere (no threats) – which means that you must be prepared to walk away (from the relationship) if your partner is not prepared to accept and acknowledge the items on your list.

For instance, if you were to say, "I need for you to respect my beliefs and feelings," then you must, in turn, respect the other person's beliefs and feelings, and so on ... because you can't GET IT if you can't GIVE IT.

Of course, your partner's list of deal-makers and deal-breakers is also subject to the same criteria.

Therefore, if two people prepare, present, and reach full agreement on their lists, they will have accomplished something that is very rare in all forms of Intimate Relationships – the creation of a mutually agreed-upon 'rule book' from which to administer their relationship. You might want to use one or several of these ideas when you approach your partner. The bottom line is that one person can work on his or her part of relationship issues, but there is much more that can be accomplished when both partners avail themselves of the process.

Note: While the solution to all human problems is 'simple', never confuse simple with 'easy'. For example, if you're an angry person, then the simple advice would be "stop being angry", which is good advice, but does not explain how to stop being angry. If great advice is all we needed, then we could just ask every person we meet to advise us – or we could just tune into Oprah or Dr. Phil.

But changing long-established behaviors is not usually an easy fix to make. And that is why in Dynamic Discovery, we show you how to switch from unwanted to wanted behaviors.

In order to gain a much deeper understanding of yourself and how to deal with and change thinking, doing, and feeling behaviors, check out our website – www.DynamicDiscovery.ca – for information about us and about our e-book, Dynamic Discovery, and the companion workbook.

Meeting Your Wants

Since what usually drives us as social beings is our wants and not our needs, we think of what we want, behave to get what we want, fantasize about what we want and so on. We can check whether we are meeting our wants through addressing three basic questions:

1. What is the greatest fear in respect to my issue?

_____

_____

_____

2. What do I want?

_____

_____

_____

3. What am I doing to get what I want?

_____

_____

_____

4. Is it working? Yes _____ No _____

Write out your answers, acknowledge them, and then get on with doing something about it ... because behind your greatest fear is your greatest weakness, and it will always come true if you obsess about it. However, behind your greatest weakness lies your greatest strength. Deal with it and get stronger; ignore it and become weaker.

Therefore, if your weakness lies within a troubled marriage, then your strength can come from learning how to deal with that particular problem ... so that you never have to go through that particular stress again. And 'dealing with' it may not involve living happily ever after with your current spouse.

What?

That's right. For many reasons, you or your partner may decide that the marriage cannot or should not be sustained. Only you have the right to decide whether to stay or go. That is your decision to make. Only yours.

Once you've gone through the process we will describe here, you will come to realize that you are the only person in the world who can change your behaviors. You will also come to realize that the best reason to make changes to your behaviors is to benefit yourself – to make your life better. If you want to be happier, you will have to take responsibility for your life. To do otherwise is to become a victim or codependent.

A New Day

You can capitalize on this opportunity to start over. All you have to do is say, "Enough! As of right now, I'm going to make a new start, and I will begin by determining which of my values and beliefs are holding me back."

Please note: to find out all you need to know about your values and beliefs and how to make change(s), go to our website www.DynamicDiscovery.ca and download the free workbook, *What Are Your Values?*

Let's Look At Our Basic Human Needs

In psychology, it is assumed that people have certain basic needs, and in our program (Dynamic Discovery) they are classified under five headings for which we apply the acronym LAFFS:

1) Love and Belonging – this includes sex, families or loved ones, as well as groups.

2) Achievement, Power and Recognition – which includes feeling worthwhile as well as winning.

3) Freedom – includes independence, autonomy, your own 'space'.

4) Fun – includes pleasure and enjoyment.

5) Survival – includes nourishment and shelter.

Whether we are aware of it or not, we are acting all the time to meet these needs, but we don't necessarily act effectively. Socializing with people is an effective way to meet our need for belonging, while isolating and self-pitying in the hope that people will come to us is generally an ineffective way of meeting that need; it is painful and costly (in psychological terms) and seems to never work in the long-term.

So if life is unsatisfactory or we are distressed or in trouble, one basic thing to check is whether we are succeeding in meeting our four (4) basic psychological needs (LAFF) – only those four because the fifth, survival, is implied – because it is in how we meet those four 'psychological' needs that we run into trouble.

Reality Check

As the roles of men and women in North American society have changed in recent decades, couples are finding it harder than ever to stay together. Census Bureau statisticians project that as many as four marriages out of every 10 taking place today will end in divorce. The marriages that survive do so not because of luck, experts say, but because of hard work and skill.

This is the age of negotiation in marriage and there are many questions that should be addressed, but let's start with three very simple ones:

1. Who pays for the movie?

_____

2. Who takes off work when a child is sick?

_____

3. Who handles the family finances?

_____

Those were the simple and easy questions. The tougher, deeper questions are sprinkled throughout this workbook.

We've gone from marriages where very little needed to be negotiated to ones where nearly everything needs to be negotiated. It's the success or failure of that negotiation that often determines the durability of relationships. That's one reason why so many couples are attending counseling, mediation, or couples' programs.

A series of polls has highlighted the challenges couples face managing careers, raising families, divvying responsibilities and keeping their individual identities intact. While changing gender roles have considerably altered the way men and women relate to each other in schools, on dates and in the workplace, in the confines of marriage and home life, the shifts have not been so dramatic. Most relevant surveys portray a North America where most married couples have the same traditional split of responsibilities that their parents and grandparents had, where men bring home most of the bacon, and women – though now powerful forces in the workplace – continue to organize and run the household.

From cooking and washing clothes to paying the bills and taking children to the doctor, women are carrying the heaviest load at home. Studies show that men are doing more around the house than they did in the past, but husbands mow lawns, shovel snow and fix toilets while wives shop for birthday presents, drop off kids at soccer practice and volunteer for the class cookie sale.

It may be that men are still able to use their greater economic power to opt out of doing work at home. Or it may be that people's preferences are in reality less egalitarian – less into equality – than we thought.

What Do You Know About Your Marriage?

1: Do We Care About Each Other As Good Friends Do?

Don't ask: "Are we in love?" The question to ask instead is: "Are we – or can we become – good friends?"

"Being in love" often means infatuation, romance, and high chemistry – things that are essentially selfish. This type of 'love' is not a good reason to get married, but friendship is.

Friendship is not selfish. Real love is about giving to and caring about another person's life.

2: Are We Emotionally Honest And Vulnerable With Each Other?

If you are unable to honestly share your feelings with your partner, it's not possible to truly connect and really feel close to that person. Being afraid to share what you feel is usually because expressing it makes you vulnerable; it's dangerous. Two people who cannot be emotionally open with each other can never enjoy true intimacy.

How do you know if the two of you are emotionally open and honest? The next time you have a conversation with your partner, ask him or her, "What do you feel about me right now?" or, "How does what I just said make you feel?" If you can communicate like this with each other consistently, you have the potential for building an intimate relationship.

3: Do We Consistently Reach Win-Win Resolutions To Our Problems?

Let's be honest: marriage is one problem after another! That doesn't sound very romantic, but it's very realistic.

Couples often mistake good chemistry for good communication. Just because you can talk for hours on the phone and feel very connected doesn't mean you have good communication.

The only way you know if you have good communication is when you have problems.

When there is a disagreement of any kind – small or large – this is when you find out how good or how bad your communication is. The essence of good communication is that you can consistently reach win-win solutions to your problems and disagreements. This means when you are finished talking, both of you feel good about the solution. There are no bad feelings on either side.

Problems that don't get fully resolved turn into resentments. And when resentments build, love departs. The problem is not the problem. The communication about the problem is the problem.

4: Do We Take Care Of Each Other's Needs?

One of the most important principles of marriage is: If it's important to you, it's important to me. Taking care of each other's needs is about wanting to give each other pleasure.

Being a giver is probably the most important character trait to have for staying married. People are naturally takers. It takes a great deal of effort to become a genuine giver. Giving in order to get something back is being a taker.

An important question to ask yourself is:

Do I enjoy giving to this person or do I find it burdensome?

_____

_____

Do you enjoy taking care of this need?

Yes _____ No _____

Consider this: Giving builds love. Taking destroys it.

5: Do We Admire And Respect Each Other?

We need to respect and admire the person we marry. We respect a person's good character, meaningful aspirations and goals he/she is committed to, and the good deeds he/she has done, not the way he/she looks.

How do you talk to each other? If you truly respect someone, you talk to that person with respect and dignity. Do you criticize or put each other down? Are you patient or impatient with each other? Do you make fun of your partner in front of others and then try to cover it by saying, "I was only joking"?

One of the biggest ways that couples demonstrate a lack of respect for each other is by playing games. Playing games is immature and childish. Mature people who respect each other don't play games. They are consistently upfront, open, and honest.

6: Do You Believe In Your Partner?

Your partner needs your respect and support and needs you to believe in her or him. People today are under so much pressure and so many demands are being made of them, so the one place none of us needs to feel more pressured is at home. Work and social problems need to stay out of the home.

The cruelest thing partners can do is nag. Give your partner your love, not your list of demands. Be upfront. And be a friend.

7: Do I Trust This Person Completely?

The emotional foundation of love is trust. Without complete trust, you can't build love. The essential issue of trust is captured in the question, "Is my partner there for me?" A solid marriage is built on solid trust. Also ask, "Can I trust that my partner will provide a safe home for my feelings and needs? Can I be sure I can be vulnerable with my partner? Am I afraid my partner will abandon, reject, or shame me?"

Then determine how you would answer if your partner asked those questions of you.

A key way to build trust is by respecting and validating another person's feelings. Listening to another person's feelings is one of the greatest acts of kindness we can perform.

If the word 'trust' has bad connotations for you, try this response if your partner asks if they can trust you: "If I do what I say I'm going to do, when I say I'm going to do it, will that be good enough?"

If doing what you say you're going to do, when you say you'll do it, isn't good enough for your partner, then the problem isn't with you; it's with your partner.

8: Do We Want The Same Things Out Of Life?

One of two things happens in a marriage: People either grow together or grow apart.

Spiritual compatibility will help you grow together because you'll be on the same page in terms of your values, priorities, and life goals.

Life's most important question is: "What am I living for?" If you cannot answer that question, you must do your research and find out, because if you don't know what you want and need, your partner will never be able to help you.

Marriage is risky. Two people who don't know what they're living for may have a difficult time growing together and staying together over the long-run.

9: Do I Have Peace Of Mind About My Actions?

To have peace of mind, you have to identify and resolve the things that bother you – in this case, the things that bother you about being married to your partner. To identify everything that bothers you, you must be ruthlessly honest with yourself and listen to your feelings ... and then identify your part in your unease.

If you don't have peace of mind about your marriage, track down the reason. If you are diligent, you'll discover the reason why you are dragging your feet.

Let that sink in...

Once you've identified everything about your partner that bothers you, it is then time to (honestly) look for your part in those particular 'botherations'. Maybe you're bothered because you see yourself in your partner's shortcomings.

For greater impact and clarity, write it out.

And if you can't track it down through your own efforts, contact us.

Those things – and many others as well – we can help you deal with. To learn more, check out www.DynamicDiscovery.ca.

Requirements For Personal Change

The basic requirement is that you need to always operate in your own Best Interest, the definition for which is as follows:

• your Best Interest is served when your plans and/or actions are not intended to be deliberately hurtful or harmful to yourself or others.

• if others choose to feel hurt, that is their choice and does not require you to do or change anything.

Superficiality has to be replaced by genuine empathy and compassion for yourself and others. Through love and caring, your emptiness, hopelessness and sense of demoralization will dissipate. Love is the sharing of your 'self', that part that is essentially you.

This sharing of your true self is essentially an act of giving of yourself without an anticipation of reward. If it becomes distorted by external demands or expectations, it becomes a superficial entity, an object, a plaything. This is not love; it is simply going through the motions of detached, robotic pretending without real involvement.

The Process Of Change

The process of change must include the following:

First, you must recognize and admit that at some level, you have exhibited hateful behavior toward others during your lifetime. You must not be in a state of denial and only point your fingers at others. You are human and all humans make mistakes.

Second, you must be honest and open in your conversations with your partner – even if your partner does not do the same.

Third, and this is the true test – where you put the pedal to the metal, where you either put up or shut up, where the true test of character is demonstrated – with regard to really and truly eliminating hurtful behaviors and resentments, you must not only 'talk the talk', but also 'walk the walk'. Actually changing your behavior is the only way you can truly get rid of unwanted feelings; it is simply not enough to only discuss them. Talking about these things is a good beginning, and teaching people to tolerate one another is another good step in the right direction. However, the real deal and the ultimate goal is to learn to love yourself and each other; and through practice, have this become your new lifestyle.

The challenge is to control or change your feelings, which is accomplished by changing your thoughts and actions. The good news is that these changes will change your attitude, because you operate as a total behavior system; see the control car and control computer discussion and illustrations on the next pages.

Control Car

Balanced Car Example

The balanced illustration below demonstrates how our thinking affects our lives. The example car is front-wheel drive. The engine represents your brain while your mind is the steering wheel.

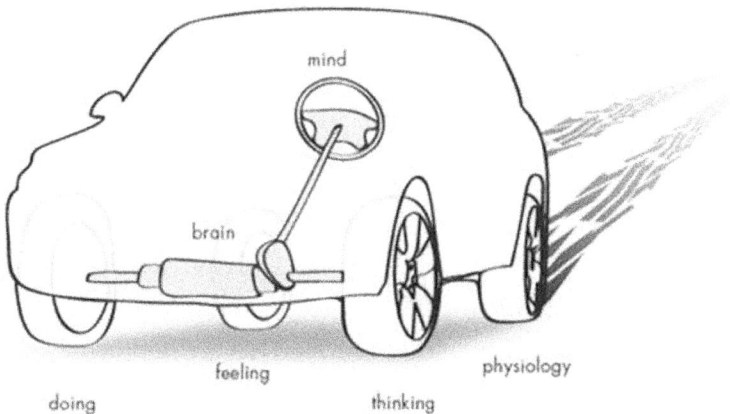

The human body is a very smart system that has never been fully duplicated. No other living thing has the power of thought and implementation that a human has, nor the ability for change and correction. A car, like the one pictured above, with well-balanced tires, will drive you properly in the direction you want to go. First, there is a thought, which is followed by feelings, actions and physiological response.

'Unbalanced' Car Example

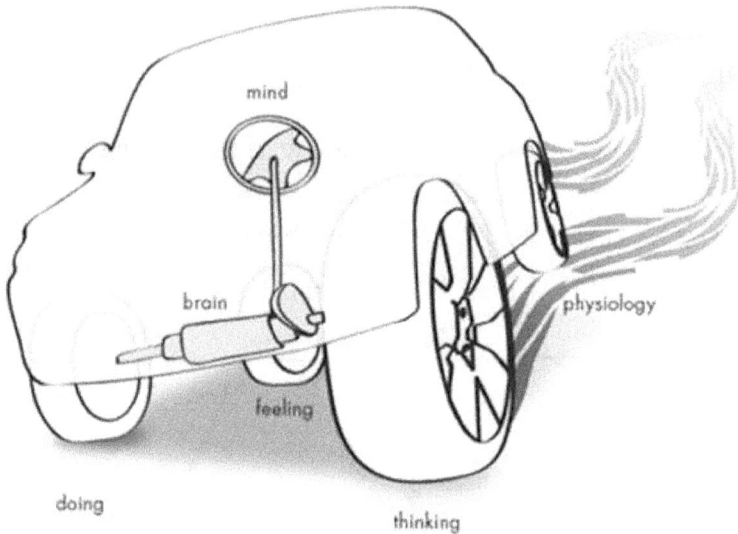

A major elevation in any of the behaviors would have the same effect as greatly overinflating that particular tire. Repression of the behavior deflates the particular tire, which may cause us to feel unbalanced.

In the unbalanced example, the thinking tire is obsessive (greatly inflated), the feelings are somewhat inflated, and the actions are somewhat deflated (one becomes less active). Done long enough and your health (physiology) could suffer. This car would not steer well – it would not be taking you in the direction you want to go.

Control Computer Theory

The way to change how we think is to change our thinking with a new 'program'. Since all change is stressful it is comforting to know that the old program will always be on our 'hard drive' (in our memory), allowing us the choice between old and new programs. If, at any time we want to revisit our old behaviors, we just have to access our memory and take a look. As well, if the new behaviors are too extreme or negative, we can replace them with another new program – totally new or blended.

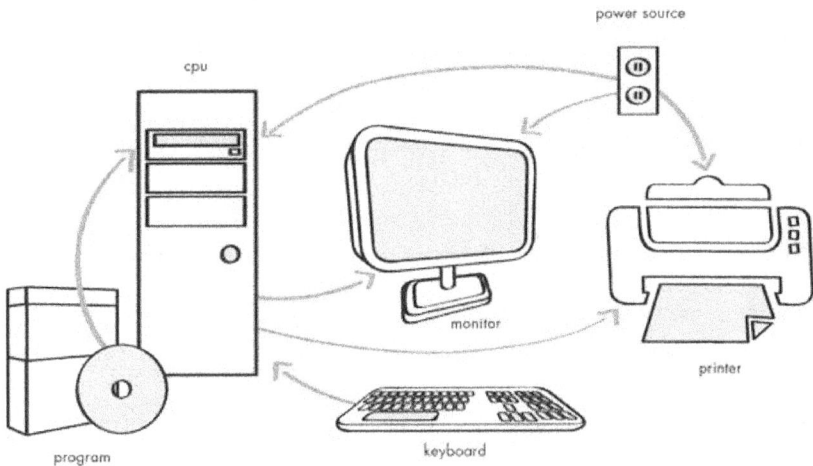

Summary

So ... we change our feelings through our thoughts and actions – which means we're not at the mercy of our emotional life. Emotions (the well from which our feelings arise) serve as a barometer of what's going on in our conscious mind. And we can change what's going on inside by consciously monitoring our thoughts.

Five Helpful Questions

Consider the state of your marriage and ask yourself:

1. What am I doing for my marriage?

_____

_____

_____

2. Is it helping me get what I want?

Yes _____ No _____

3. If not, what might be some other thing(s) I could try?

_____

_____

_____

4. Which idea will I try first?

_____

5. When can I start?

_____

Four Simple Steps

Our thoughts affect our actions and feelings – which, in turn, creates our attitude. And the best way to monitor our thoughts is by listening to our self-talk. In other words, we need to think about our thinking.

We have the ability to consider our thought process and not just react by instinct. And since we can control our thoughts, we have the ability to influence our feelings and thus change our attitude.

That is good news indeed ... because in four simple steps, you can change your thoughts, feelings and actions:

1. Identify the unwanted thought, feeling and/or action you want to change and write it here:

_____

_____

2. Identify the wanted thought, feeling and/or action you want to incorporate in its place:

_____

_____

3. Pay conscious attention. Each time you become aware of yourself using the undesired thought, feeling and/or action, note that fact. Simply note that you are doing it. Avoid criticizing or judging yourself.

4. Continue to check on your thoughts, feelings and/or actions and take note whenever you find yourself behaving in the old way.

As you note this, stop yourself immediately and consciously replace the thought, feeling and/or action with the new thought, feeling and/or action. Continue this process until the old thought, feeling and/or action have become integrated.

The key to being successful is to choose only one thought, feeling and/or action at a time – avoid overwhelming yourself by choosing two, three or four issues. Work on only one and when it is integrated, choose another and so on, until you are satisfied with all your thoughts, feelings and/or actions.

1. Fulfilling Your Human Potential

Dating, marriage, family and friendships are important stages in our lives.

By successfully forming loving relationships with other people, we are able to experience love and intimacy.

Those who fail to form lasting relationships may feel isolated and alone.

Full potential = self-fulfillment, the tendency to become everything that one is capable of becoming.

You have within you a potential that is a fundamental part of your existence. This involves an inherent yearning or drive toward health, growth and becoming a fulfilled human being.

After your basic human needs are met, it is a good time to press toward good values: kindness, love, unselfishness, courage and goodness. These characteristics help formulate the real definition of a fulfilled person.

The ability to love through the sharing of your 'self' starts with giving and evolves into a mutual emotional merging with another human being. This is the extraordinary experience of pure, unselfish love.

Unfortunately, for various reasons, starting with the early trauma of separateness and isolation, we often become misguided in our lives and pursue lifestyles that direct us away from our more fundamental, positive growth potential. In certain religious terms, these types of lifestyles are often motivated by the seven deadly sins – also referred to as 'capital vices' because they engender other sins, other vices or cardinal sins, and are a classification of vices (part of Christian ethics) that has been used since early Christian times to educate and instruct Christians concerning fallen humanity's tendency to sin. These sins are usually referred to as the seven deadly sins and are wrath, greed, sloth, pride, lust, envy, and gluttony.

Whether or not you agree with the above-noted Christian ethics, you can likely agree that those seven 'behaviors' are unhealthy and unhelpful. And when one or more or all of those seven behaviors are 'seasoned' with one or more or all of the five foundations of conflict – control, power, money, jealousy and/or sex – you have a very explosive mix.

You can see that arguing from a position of pride and lust combined with power and jealousy can only lead to either damaged feelings or a collapse of the relationship ... because all of those behaviors are controlling and the opposite of real love and open-mindedness.

Many of us, instead of living a life of intimacy and loving involvement with other people, become locked into a protective, defensive lifestyle where we simply go through the motions of being a real person. We play a pretend game, relating with phony emotions, vacuous comments and empty intimacies, which are poor substitutes for an authentic relationship.

Do you do any of the above behaviors?

Yes _____ No _____

Now name the behavior or behaviors that you have used and how you have used it or them:

_____

_____

_____

_____

_____

_____

If you are not living a life of intimacy and loving involvement with other people, the next step is to become even more isolated and withdrawn into a life of emptiness, hopelessness and demoralization. You may try to offset this predicament through drugs, alcohol, sex or other forms of consumption or obsession in order to mask your inner struggle involving detachment and isolation. On the outside, you may look okay, but on the inside you would be an empty shell.

If that's the case, it's not too late ... it's never too late to turn your life around.

An effective way to turn your life around is to take stock of the reality of your life and be grateful for what you do have – even though you want more or different – because it is difficult (if not impossible) to feel depressed, resentful or internally ugly when you adopt an attitude of gratitude.

2. Taking Responsibility For Your 'Self'

Owning your 'self' involves taking personal responsibility for what you do. Part of being a mature, responsible adult is to know that when you make a decision in life, you alone are responsible for the outcome. You. Not someone else. When something goes wrong, you need not look beyond yourself to lay the blame – only, instead of blaming, you can use the event or happening as a learning experience.

It's no secret that the answer to a bad attitude is a good laugh, a smile, and pleasant thoughts – because you can't genuinely laugh and smile without a corresponding good feeling. Your feelings and actions have a direct impact on your outward demeanor.

Once the basics for survival – food, clothing and shelter – are catered for, humans have other more complex psychological needs – such as the need to love and be loved, the need to belong, the need for power, self-worth, freedom, and happiness. Each of us has these needs, but some need more of one thing than another. What makes it harder is that, often, you are not actually aware of exactly what it is that you need.

For our purposes, the word 'love' refers to a variety of different feelings, states, and attitudes that range from interpersonal affection ("I love my mother") to pleasure ("I loved that meal"). It can refer to an emotion of a strong attraction and personal attachment. It can also be a virtue representing human kindness, compassion, and affection – 'the unselfish loyal and benevolent concern for the good of another'. It may also describe compassionate and affectionate actions towards other humans, one's self or animals.

Love may be understood as a function to keep human beings together against menaces and to facilitate the continuation of the species.

There is an old saw that says there is a thin line between love and hate – therefore, love is giving someone the power to destroy you, and trusting them not to.

However, love is the most precious activity of a mature human being. Love is not merely an emotion, but an attitude and how we relate to ourselves, other people and the world around us. True love involves compassion, caring and giving.

Our major premise is that you are responsible for your own choices, decisions, goals, and the general degree of happiness in your life. Our intention here is to help you understand why and how you make the choices that determine the course of your life, recognizing:

• You have freedom to make choices.

• You have the knowledge to understand how to make choices.

• You have sufficient power and control to make choices.

• You must take responsibility for your choices ... for you are the only person on Earth who can make a choice for change.

• Your Behavior should be considered in its totality: thinking, doing, feeling, and physiology.

• You already have the capacity to change within you.

• You do not have to be a victim ... unless you choose to be.

Full awareness should be your goal so that you can become all that you can be. You learned most of what you know about intimate relationships through your early experiences in your family. Your personal history has a great deal of influence on what happens in your current relationships – on your behavior, your feelings, your expectations. You can change these influences if you become aware of them and want to. Creating and then sustaining a pleasurable intimate relationship does not work by magic, but depends upon a certain set of skills and understandings. It is well worthwhile to conduct an inventory of what you have inherited, keeping what fits for today and changing what does not.

If your goal is a relationship that both partners can live with joyfully, each partner must become able to identify his or her own feelings and needs, and learn to communicate them in such a way that they can get met. This means communicating one's needs and desires without making the other partner feel resentful, smothered, burdened, manipulated, or inadequate. Our Dynamic Discovery program will show you a number of skills that will help you to change your behavior, attitudes, and feelings in ways that contribute to this goal.

One skill you can develop is how to change the way you think so as to change the way you act and feel. You might well ask, "Why would I want to change the way I think?" The answer is simply this: if you are not getting what you want (from your life), then you will have to change what you are doing. As Albert Einstein said, "Insanity is doing the same thing over and over again and expecting different results."

So ... if you want to change anything, you must do something different. It doesn't matter whether the change is to a human behavior, or a recipe for pound cake. Doing something different will produce a change to the outcome. Consider this ... if I am an angry person and the net effect is to drive everyone away from me, and if I don't like being isolated and/or lonely, then the answer is to change, to do something different. And I do it for me. Because I want something my current behaviors are not providing.

Another thing for you to know is that all human problems have simple solutions – not necessarily easy, just simple. To clarify, when I say simple I mean "not complex". For instance, if you're having trouble with alcohol, the simple solution is to stop drinking. Every alcohol abuser has heard this advice many times, and has rejected it many times. Why would an alcoholic reject what is the right answer? They reject it because it doesn't tell the alcoholic 'how' to stop drinking. And the 'how' is seldom easy. (A dictionary definition of 'easy' is requiring little effort, free from pain, discomfort, trouble, or worry.)

We fear what we do not know and, because fear is a very strong human emotion, there may be discomfort no matter what change you undertake. Pain, however, is optional.

For example, if you had creditors chasing you, then every knock on the door or every phone call could represent a creditor and you might conjure up all kinds of scary and horrific scenarios ... before you open the door or answer the phone. The reason for this is because the mind is amazingly powerful and has the ability to create concepts. Concepts become perceptions and perception truly is reality, for the human body cannot tell the difference between emotions resulting from a fabrication of the mind and an actual event.

It is very useful to move towards solutions rather than away from problems, because often the quickest way to find a solution is just to charge right at it, rather than pussyfooting around, getting all anxious and fretful.

So ... what if a few simple questions could help you look at your problems and difficulties differently? What if these questions could help find solutions and gain a glimmer of hope? They can. And it all starts with a simple question:

• What do I want? (be specific)

_____

_____

_____

From that question, others follow:

- What is that going to do for me?

_____

_____

_____

- What's stopping me?

_____

_____

_____

- What's important to me here?

_____

_____

_____

- What's working well?

_____

_____

- What can be better?

_____

_____

_____

• What resources are going to support me?

_____

_____

_____

Working Toward A Solution

Because the questions previously asked may or may not lead you to the beginnings of a solution, the following question may get you thinking in the right direction:

> Suppose tonight, while you are asleep, something magical happens. Because you were asleep, you didn't know it had happened, but everything you ever wanted is now there. You now have your perfect life. When you waken in the morning, how will you be able to tell that the 'magic' as happened?

To carry out this exercise, sit or lie down somewhere quiet where you won't be disturbed. Allow your breathing to slow, settle comfortably, and let your mind wander where it will. Relative to the 'Suppose' question, ask yourself:

• What will I see that is different?

_____

_____

_____

• What will I hear that is different?

_____

_____

_____

• What will I feel inside that is different from the way I feel now?

_____

_____

• What will I be that is different?

_____

_____

_____

By answering those specific questions, you will begin to see what it is that you are missing, what it is that you want.

3. Five Targets

The following five topics all weave together and build upon one another.

1) Dealing

2) Managing Your Problems

3) Your 'Self'

4) Pleasuring

5) Expectancies

Please keep track of your responses to the questions included in each topic since when they are taken together you will see how your natural responses affect your relationships.

1) Dealing

In order to know and nurture both yourself and your partner so that you can recognize, acknowledge, and even enjoy your differences rather than seeing them as a threat or an attack, it is important to learn how to enjoy your partner and to sustain your relationship as a continuing source of mutual pleasure. You started that process by working on your deal-makers and deal-breakers back on page 8.

We do not get into trouble in our marriages because we're weak or stupid; we get into trouble for one or more of the following:

• we think that whatever it is that we believe in will be accepted by our partners ...because we're in love;

• we feel that marriage is a natural destination for couples in love, so we believe that a good relationship will just happen;

• we think that although our partner has some rather bizarre habits, we find them to be cute little behaviors... until they become overwhelmingly annoying;

• or any one of a hundred (or a thousand) other 'reasons'.

Or you can boil it down and understand that conflict usually involves issues of Control and/or Power and/or Money and/or Jealousy and/or Sex – and is often expressed as a dispute between two or more people, based on their Feelings.

So ... which of the following issues are involved in or are governing your disputes:

• Control ____

• Power ____

• Money ____

• Jealousy ____

• Sex ____

Please be aware that the five "issues" noted above are Feelings, and the problem with arguments based on Feelings is that Feelings involve Perception, and Perception is an expression of your Values and Beliefs, and your Values and Beliefs are your 'Truth'. And if your truths and your partner's truths are not the same ... well, then, the two of you go to war... because your truth is the only truth, which makes you 'right'. And your partner's truth leads them into the same arena. And then the two of you fight ... to the death ... of your relationship.

So how do you get over arguments?

You don't have to get over them – they are part of the PAST... and the past is over! What's important is the MEANING the past has for you NOW. And the meaning of your past is determined by your actions in the future.

What's to be done? Well, we will get to that. Eventually.

For now, consider and make note of your answers to which feeling issues are involved in or are governing your disputes, because they will come into play in the next topics.

2) Managing Your Problems

A dear friend has provided me with the following information concerning her own marriage:

> "We started our marriage in excitement, hope, and good feelings, with perhaps a measure of fear mixed in. Our history was yet to evolve, so the beginning was more a time of romance than reality. But no lasting connection is built on a steady string of good times because relationships, like individuals, deepen by meeting the hard times head on, by not accepting defeat, and by using every difficulty as a learning and growth experience. By working together to solve our problems – those things we did not want or choose in our lives – we became stronger.
>
> Looking back, we appreciate the richness of our lives together because we have risen above our problems, grown from them, and had many times of fun and pleasure. Our problems were hard, but built our relationship."

Of course, I must remind you that problems not dealt with – left unsolved – make us weaker.

Good communication happens when you are able to:

• recognize when your style of communication is more of a problem than the problem you are communicating about;

• avoid the mind-reading that so often leads to misunderstandings with your partner, by checking out your assumptions before you act on them and by not expecting your partner to know without being told;

• learn how to make sure that each partner is being heard by the other, using the processes of empathic listening and shared meaning;

• communicate all of your feelings (including anger) without destroying love, by learning to accept and express those feelings comfortably, directly, and non-destructively;

• recognize and deal with covert, indirect expressions of anger, or a fight-phobic partner, or an aggressively hostile partner;

• learn how to clear the air of strong fear, pain, or anger before attempting to resolve conflicts or solve problems;

• fight in such a way that you actually resolve the issue at hand, including problems related to sex, money, children, time, in-laws, ex-spouses, your home, housework, fidelity, and jealousy.

George Bissett

Talking

Talking is an art.

Let me explain.

Effective communication – the accurate sharing of significant information about each other – is the cement that holds a relationship together, permitting both partners to build upon what each has to contribute until they've created a unique structure that is different from and bigger than the sum of its parts. Just as two rope-climbers, respecting each other's skills, can belay and secure each other to scale a mountain that neither could climb alone, so trusted lines of communication can enable both partners to discover and activate hidden potential in themselves, their partners and their relationship.

You're always 'communicating' in some fashion, of course, and couldn't survive otherwise. But qualitative growth and fulfillment requires that you learn to communicate accurately – not only about the practical realities of the objective world, but also about the subjective realities of your inner world – your feelings and perceptions, hopes and fears, values and goals. To do so, you must:

• have sufficient self-awareness and self- do feel/believe/want – that is, know what message you want to send;

• have sufficient self-acceptance and self-confidence to take the risk of disclosing what's inside without being absolutely certain that your partner will understand; and

• be able to use all of the verbal and non-verbal signals necessary to transmit that message so clearly that it means precisely the same thing to your partner as it does to you.

Even in the best of situations, when your partner shares your desire to communicate in this fashion, there are many potential pitfalls:

• some words, especially those dealing with subjective states and feelings, have many shades of meaning;

• some kinds of experiences and feelings simply cannot be adequately described by words alone.

Most of us have fallen into the habit of using words as weapons (for attack or defense) rather than as tools (for the sharing of information); and unless we really do know what we're feeling and are prepared to be honest about it, we can unconsciously confuse the issue by sending contradictory messages – with the words 'saying' one thing while our tone or facial expression or body posture says another. This usually happens when, for whatever reason, our self-esteem is low enough to make it impossible for us to be 'straight' with ourselves.

George Bissett

Listening

Many of these problems can be overcome by employing certain techniques – and the first technique is Listening – with an eye to being happy rather than right.

Half of the dialogue process depends on how the 'sender' gets in touch with and transmits all of the data that he/she has (perceptions, feelings, expectations, needs) that might be relevant to a given transaction with his/her partner. But it takes two to communicate. Both partners equally share the responsibility for ensuring that clear messages get sent and received.

In the first place, of course, functional conversations seldom take the form of a series of uninterrupted monologues, especially if the issue is a significant one for both parties – which is precisely when you most need communication skills. Rather, they are lively, if not heated, dialogues – and they should be.

The process of risking and sharing and learning is exciting and demanding, but that doesn't mean that dialogues need to be competitive, one-way exchanges. To the extent that real information is exchanged and reflected upon and incorporated into the relationship and the situation, both parties 'win'. To the extent that it isn't, both parties lose. So both parties must genuinely want to receive as well as give information, and both must do all in their power – by their manner and tone as well as their words – to facilitate the accurate exchange of honest messages. They must truly want to know what the other is experiencing and feeling and needing. If they do truly want to know, this will inevitably be reflected in their manner – in their concern for the other; in the respect with which they attend to what the other has to say; in the way their responses reflect that they have heard and have taken what they've heard into account; in the way that they use both their own and their partner's words as tools rather than as weapons; in the way that they respect whatever 'differences' emerge rather than being offended or frightened by them – in short, in all the ways they reflect their basic esteem for and trust in both themselves and their partner. Fortunately, there is one reasonably simple, though demanding, technique for accomplishing all of this, and that is through actually and consciously listening.

We seldom, if ever, really 'listen' to another person, except for quite egocentric reasons: we listen to that which is of practical use to us (a stock market tip or a tax loophole); we listen to that which embellishes our own interests or skills (a lecture or a new way of

preparing hollandaise sauce); we listen for that which flatters our self-esteem (agrees with our own views); and we listen for plausible opportunities to jump back into the conversation to push our own opinions. This is quite normal. In fact, humankind mightn't have survived as a species if we hadn't been so thoroughly egocentric. But it doesn't promote the kind of listening that permits you to zero in on what the words mean to the speaker, as opposed to the more self-centered value they might have for you.

The kind of listening referred to above means focusing on the speaker with an intensity that excludes virtually all other awareness, appreciating their emotions and body language as well as listening to their words. It means putting yourself in your partner's shoes so thoroughly that you:

• grasp why the topic is important to your partner;

• feel why your partner chooses each particular word;

• imagine how your partner feels in that situation, that mood, and that chair;

• picture what you look like to your partner, what signals your partner is picking up even as he or she speaks.

In this way, you begin to get an appreciation of how what your partner is saying relates to what is going on inside of him or her.

You have the capacity to listen in this way, but until you've practiced it for a while, it takes considerable effort. The results are more than worth it, however – because you not only hear more but, because you're attending to all of the cues and signals, your understanding is infinitely more accurate.

The fact that you are making the effort, are truly listening, is shown in a thousand subtle ways that you couldn't possibly program or fake. The tone and pitch of each word, the timing and nuance of each nod, smile or raised eyebrow, the precise wording of each question or comment, tells your partner that you're really grappling with their meaning and feelings.

Since there is nothing rarer or more flattering than really being listened to, the speaker can't resist the need to be more responsible and honest in formulating and expressing their thoughts. And since it feels so good to be listened to, the speaker is far more likely to return the favor when it is your turn to speak.

True conversation is a partnership, an orchestration – not a competition. Pitted against an expert non-listener, an articulate speaker becomes dull.

If you're an ordinarily inarticulate person, when stimulated and encouraged and reinforced by a true listener, you can discover depths of feeling and expressiveness you never knew you had. Intimacy cannot grow without this kind of communication.

And this kind of communication must be a mutual effort: while one is baring their soul and taking risks by sharing what they uncover, the other is showing genuine respect for the speaker and the process – by listening with the greatest intensity possible. In so doing, both are showing, and not merely professing, their trust in and respect for each other – and because they both thereby get in tune with each other's subtleties and complexities of meaning, they both avoid making the common mistakes of assuming that they know what the other is or means or wants, and of attributing to the other person their own beliefs and feelings.

By following the exercise, both partners acquire the ability to recognize and appreciate and deal objectively with the differences that exist between them – and from there, they can learn how to make these differences occasions for mutual growth and pride rather than divisiveness and fear.

One consequence of genuine communication, of course, is that each partner gets in touch with the 'reality' rather than the polite fiction of the other. And since no two people are going to have precisely the same wants, needs, values and beliefs, certain differences make conflict possible. Most of the differences can be resolved by adjustments and compromise; some may call for mature recognition of the fact that, in a particular area, each can pursue different ends without harming the relationship. A few may not permit either ready compromise or separate paths – those may be more appropriately dealt with using the fair fight and behavioral contracting techniques. But first, let's focus on the process of clear and congruent communication.

Listening and Talking Exercise

Start by sitting across from your partner in the congruent communication position (face-to-face, eye-to-eye, knee-to-knee, hand-to-hand). Your partner says what they have to say – in pieces small enough so that you can repeat each piece back. If what you have said is correct, your partner will acknowledge that and go on. If it is not correct, or if it is not what your partner meant, your partner will restate what they have said, and you will reflect it back again.

Repeat these steps until the speaker feels understood. Then the speaker thanks the listener and makes physical contact with them by touching their hand or giving them a hug.

An actual exchange could go something like this:

Choose a non-threatening topic and say something like, *"One thing I believe is true about me that you probably don't know is..."*

It is important that you note the following:

• When you are the speaker, be clear and concise, and say only a short paragraph before letting the listener partner echo back. If you get confused about what you are trying to say, take a quiet moment to stop, look inside and get clear with yourself what message you want the listener to receive. If the listener asks you to repeat what you have said, repeat it as exactly as possible; don't change what you said in the process of repeating it.

• If you are the listener and the speaker says too much for you to remember, say so. The listener should use words similar to those of the speaker. Using your own words for what you think the speaker is saying is called translation, and may leave the speaker feeling that what you repeat back is not quite what they said or meant. If you don't hear the speaker, perhaps because your own thoughts or feelings intrude, ask them to repeat what they have said. When the speaker is finished with all they have to say, show empathy for what you hear. Validate in a statement that you understand your partner's feelings, for example, "I can understand that ... I can see that ... It makes sense to me that..."

At first, this process feels slow and cumbersome to those of us who are used to conversations which move quickly from one topic to another, and where each partner fills in what is not said from their past experiences. But when we are under stress, because feelings are high or self-worth is low, this process is a good one to keep us on track. It requires the speaker to be clear, and stops the listener from running their own thoughts while the speaker is talking. The usual result of this process is that the speaker feels really understood, and the listener often hears something they hadn't noticed before.

Please Pay Attention To The Following:

If you think that this process is too time-consuming and/or laborious, please consider this:

Whether you are on the brink of divorce or are merely interested in improving your relationship, you have probably spent many, many hours in useless and/or damaging conversations and/or arguments that resolved nothing. So, if that's true, then devoting a very small amount of time to learn a new and productive communication process is a very small price to pay. Unless you are more interested in being right than in being happy.

When you have finished, thank your partner for listening by saying something like, "Thank you for listening to me talk about _____. I feel that you were really listening." Touch their hand, give them a hug, or some other physical contact. Then change roles and let your partner be the speaker.

It's surprising how difficult that skill is for people, because we have an extroverted society. We want to get our message across. Our message. When the other person is talking, we're thinking about our response. So that we can hammer our message home. So that we can prove our 'rightness'.

To be clear, you have to confide with honesty. Without fear.

You can be clear by using 'I' statements to let your partner know how you feel. You can complain without blaming so as to manage conflict with graciousness and gentleness.

One of the biggest stumbling blocks in your marriage may be individual differences, because you may not have learned to manage those differences. Some problems stem from the different ways in which you and your partner grew up. You both bring different family patterns, traditions and myths to your relationship. This communication process will change your response to the past so you can keep what works and discard what no longer works.

It's important that couples learn about physical closeness and emotional openness – to learn to have pleasure together in a non-sexual way, such as laughing together and hugging. Men who don't know how to use their strong bodies to give support and security can take comfort in the fact that it's real easy to learn. It's a lot easier to learn than golf – and it can help couples to be more aware of how teachings and experiences from our past still influence us in a negative way.

Another stumbling block is dirty fighting, where couples adopt the strategy to win or control the fight rather than negotiate a solution. Failure to communicate — not listening and not confiding — is another problem.

You don't have to be in a troubled relationship in order to improve your communication skills so as to enhance all your relationships. When that happens, there's more peace and affection at home and couples are more tender with each other.

Many couples spend very little 'quality' time together, so sometimes we have to look at our priorities. If your marriage isn't your top priority then ... well, that may be the primary problem. Maybe what the family really needs is for the parents to have some 'alone' time. For instance, you may be able to trade or swap some chores with family, friends or neighbors to allow you to spend a couple hours alone with each other, learning how to communicate and problem-solve – because by the time the kids are grown and gone, the intimacy could also be gone.

Couples can be more companionable with each other, even if they pride themselves on a pretty good relationship. This process can also improve co-operation and playfulness.

3) Your 'Self'

Your own 'self' is well-served when you have:

a. traced the **emotional history** of your family to discover which family models influence the way you relate to your partner now;

b. learned how to **take responsibility** for your current behaviors – which are a reflection of your own emotional history and your life-experiences – because it is those (current) behaviors which influence your relationships today;

c. learned about your **basic human needs** and why they sabotage your relationships when left un serviced;

d. **self-evaluated your 'self'** and learned how to treat yourself as you need to be treated;

e. **recognized your roles** in your relationships and become intimately acquainted with the richness and complexity of your own unique personality.

It is important to examine your emotional history because it really is not 'yours'; it is what you learned from those around you when you were young and impressionable. You may ask why this is important and the answer is simply this:

Anything that has been learned can be unlearned. If you can learn to behave one way, then that is the proof that you can learn to behave another way. That's all that change is – learning a positive and helpful behavior to replace a behavior that is negative and unproductive.

Think of it this way...

The way to break a habit is to replace it with another habit.

a. Emotional history

Upon reflection, you may find that you have blamed all of your problems on your upbringing – on the care, or lack thereof, provided by your parents during childhood.

Many people who are experiencing long-term behavioral problems often trace their problems to incidents involving something a parent did or said that was so significant or traumatic to them at that time of their life that their very personality was altered.

In most cases, the incidents involved the Mother. Although this seems on the surface like a major indictment of Motherhood, it makes some sense since mothers are usually the primary caregivers during the essential formative years of childhood and mothers generally have great concern for the safety and well-being of their kids, and often they try to protect them through controlling behaviors, such as guilt.

This is not to say that most parents deliberately set out to ruin the lives of their children. In fact, most parents want more for their kids than they themselves had. And, not surprisingly, most parents have a very fixed idea of what they want their kids to be and do – regardless of what the kids want. So ... our fears and concerns often get projected onto our kids.

We think because they are our kids, they must want what we want for them. And if they disappoint us, it must be because they don't understand how much we as parents have invested in them emotionally. So if they really loved me (or us), they would do whatever it took to make us proud. Therefore, the application of sufficient guilt and other punishment is often called for.

See? Someone else is to blame. Always.

How ludicrous is that?

However, the past is merely the source of your wants and of your ways of behaving. Not only are the bad things that happened to you in your past actually in your past, but your successes are there, too. Your focus should be, instead, is to on learning what needs to be learned about the past and then moving on to empowering yourself to satisfy your needs and wants now and in the future – through the knowledge that it is your perceptions that influence your behaviors.

You are a product of the past, but you do not have to be its victim.

b. Taking responsibility

Should we teach people to take responsibility for their own actions – regardless of the hand they were dealt in life? To be responsible for their own actions even when there is someone else to blame?

Maybe if we took responsibility for our own thoughts and actions, we could learn to feel better about our own lives, and about ourselves. Maybe if we learned to act according to our own Best Interest, we wouldn't keep suffering from crippling guilt, anxiety, inferiority, or try to drink, drug or excessively eat our problems away.

But by the time most of us become aware that our compensating behaviors aren't working, we're generally parents ourselves, and we may have had one or more intimate relationships that have been destroyed because of our inappropriate or ineffective behaviors.

If you're feeling a distance with the people around you – whether you have withdrawn or they have withdrawn – the surest way to bring people closer may be to change your own behavior. And in order to effect change, it is at this point where responsibility for your own self should come into it. This is where you get to pick your own direction and discover what and who you want to be ... as long as you remember that you will always experience what you create.

You might ask, "Why should I be the one to change?" and the answer is, "If you don't like what's happening, you are the only one who can change how you feel about it."

Let that sink in...

The human being is the only creature on earth that is not a prisoner of its programming, but the master of it. That means you are the only one who can do what has to be done to make yourself happy.

Nobody else. You.

Therefore, none of us needs to live even a minute longer as we are, because we have been endowed with the ability to change ourselves.

And you can do it.

So ... do what you want, as long as what you want isn't deliberately hurtful or harmful to either yourself or anyone else. Do things to help yourself, not to hurt others.

c. Your basic human needs

You were born with specific basic needs that, if left unmet, lead to disharmony or disturbance. We describe those basic human needs as follows:

Love and Belonging – to a family, to a community, or to other loved ones.

Achievement, Power and Recognition – a sense of winning or achieving or a sense of self-worth.

Freedom – to be independent, maintain your own personal space; autonomy.

Fun – to achieve satisfaction, enjoyment and a sense of pleasure.

Survival – basic needs of shelter, food, clothing and sexual fulfillment.

In order to address your five basic needs, ask yourself:

1. What is it I want?

_____

_____

_____

2. What am I doing to get what I want?

_____

_____

_____

3. Is it working? (Yes) _____ (No) _____

4. Who are the most important people in my life?

_____

_____

_____

5. What are my most deeply held values?

_____

_____

_____

6. If I become the person I would ideally like to be, what traits or characteristics would I have?

_____

_____

_____

7. What is an accomplishment that I am really proud of?

_____

_____

_____

8. If I could have the perfect job, what would that be?

_____

_____

_____

9. If I was independently wealthy, what would I do with my time?

_____

_____

10. What does it mean to be a friend?

_____

_____

_____

11. What brings a significant amount of meaning to my life?

_____

_____

_____

12. What, for me, makes a house a home?

_____

_____

_____

13. What would my Ideal World look like?

_____

_____

_____

14. What would I have to do to achieve it?

_____

_____

_____

d. Self-evaluate your 'self'

Everybody needs a certain amount of control to meet their needs for power, belonging, freedom and fun. The most important word to notice here is 'everybody'.

Control is all around you. You need a certain amount of control. Your partner needs a certain amount of control. The boss needs a certain amount of control, but so does the worker. The parent needs a certain amount of control, but so does the child. The customer needs a certain amount of control, but so does the shopkeeper.

When you fail to recognize that your partner also has a need for control, the stage is set for conflict. If, however, you are willing to negotiate and compromise, you can find ways to co-operate and create a better life.

Sometimes we ask for what we want. This respects the sense of control of both parties. Sometimes instead of asking, we demand what we want. But demanding what we want ignores the other person's sense of control and they will want to resist us.

e. Recognizing your role

Basic philosophy and assumptions:

• Change is constant and inevitable

• You are your own expert and you can define your own goals

• You have resources and strengths to solve problems

• You can self-evaluate what is possible and changeable

Emotions are a wonderful, immediate and 'alive' source of information about how you're doing and whether you're happy with what's going on in your life. But it is very, very hard to change your emotions directly.

It is easier to change your thinking – to decide, for example, that you'll no longer think of yourself as a victim; that you'll concentrate on thinking about what you can do rather than what everybody else ought to do.

Changing what you think and do is the key to changing how you feel and to getting what you want. Once you know how you think, and why you think the way you do, it is possible to change the way you think.

Let that sink in...

Only if you know how and why you think the way you do can you change how and what you think.

If you want to change anything, you absolutely must do something different. It doesn't matter whether the change is to a human behavior or a recipe for cake. Doing something different will produce a change to the outcome.

Consider this: If you're an angry person and drive people away, but you don't like being isolated and/or lonely, the answer is to change or to do something different, so the outcome is that people aren't driven away anymore.

Can you change the way you think? The answer is yes!

You can change the way you think by reprogramming the 'messaging', and isolating the reality of the situation, and getting rid of all of the garbage fantasy projection.

How do you do that?

By writing it down. Write down what you want to become. Seeing your thoughts on paper makes them real and also acts as a way to filter out what isn't or wasn't real. Repetition (practice) allows you to become what you are capable of becoming because beliefs have the power to create and the power to destroy. You have the ability to take your life experiences and create something that makes you either stronger or weaker ... all depending on your attitude. Same process, different outcomes.

Finally, consider this...

We all come in different shapes and sizes. We all have strengths and weaknesses. What's right for one person may not be right for another. There are things that are important to me that you don't care about at all. And sometimes your behavior doesn't make any sense to me.

I know I can't expect you to want the same things that I want. We are not the same person, so we will not always see things the same way. I have my own thoughts and my own ideas – that may or may not fit into your vision of who I should be.

By learning more about your own personality, you can come to a better understanding of your strengths and weaknesses. You can improve your interpersonal relationships, realign your expectations towards others, and gain a better self-knowledge that will help you define and achieve goals.

4) Pleasuring Exercise

The goal here is:

• to learn the differences between affection, comfort, bonding, sensuality, and sexuality – so that sex is not your only avenue to closeness.

• to satisfy your biological need for that combination of physical closeness and emotional openness we call Bonding, which is known as the heart of intimacy.

• to be able to communicate openly and honestly about your sexual and sensual needs and to get them met.

To start, begin at the beginning by individually determining what you want to learn about yourself and then jointly deciding what you want to learn about your partner.

By understanding your own sexual desires and responses, you can then guide your partner.

Because it is not a race or a competition, the approach is:

1. Be caring and constructive.

2. Feedback is only positive and focused on what is liked and desirable so as to replace what is not liked or is unwanted. Replace unwanted with wanted.

3. Be specific about requests for change – if you can't describe exactly what you want, then your partner may not be able to accommodate you.

4. When requesting change, focus solely on the wanted positive.

5. Be supportive: emotional and sexual change is more easily accomplished when the atmosphere is positive – no threats, demands or coercion.

6. Agree on how much time to spend on the exercises.

Many sexual difficulties stem from superficial causes. If a sexual difficulty is rooted in a lack of knowledge, for example, information and instruction may be all that are needed to treat it. If the trouble is of recent origin, a series of guided sexual tasks may be enough to change patterns of response.

Helping couples develop a sexual style that integrates intimacy and eroticism positions a couple as an intimate sexual team, rather than being stuck in the traditional power struggle of men emphasizing eroticism and intercourse frequency and women emphasizing intimacy and affectionate touch. Many women see his erection as a demand for intercourse, so they don't engage in touching unless they want to have sex. This is a loss for her, him, and their intimate relationship.

What follows is an exercise to enhance non-demand sexuality. Non-demand pleasuring involves affectionate, sensual, playful, and erotic touching both inside and outside the bedroom, which creates an empowering understanding that not all touching can or should lead to intercourse.

Most importantly, begin the exercise in a manner that facilitates sexual comfort and pleasure for both of you.

Communicating Alternatives

Start by discussing your feelings about non-demand touching. Be aware of when and how you feel pressure that diminishes spontaneity and playfulness during a sexual encounter. Remember, in this exercise there is no demand involved; your desires and choices are what count.

During this discussion, develop and refine a 'signal system' that tells your partner whether you want to proceed to intercourse. This communication may be verbal, like saying, "I really want to make love," "I'm not in the mood to make love," "Let's get it on," "Let me just hold you," or "I've enjoyed this; let it be." The communication could also be nonverbal — for example, massaging your partner's genitals and switching to an intercourse position, moving to sensuous pleasuring, using eye contact to say 'yes' or 'no', or moving your partner's hands to or from your genitals. Your partner can answer with a signal that says, "Okay" or "Not tonight: let's just play." Don't stop at saying or signaling "No." Suggest something you would like to engage in instead: a backrub, just talking and holding each other, taking a sensuous bath, giving manual or oral sex, taking a walk, cuddling and going to sleep. Pleasure-oriented touching, not sexual performance, is the key to couple intimacy.

Begin this exercise nude in your bedroom. Lying on the bed, the woman should position herself behind her partner with their entire bodies touching – her chest to his back, her knees bent inside his, her arms around his body while he holds her hands. This is a nice position in which to lie together and feel close and connected. He is in a protected and passive position, allowing himself to feel cared for.

In this scenario, it is the woman's prerogative to indicate whether she wants to extend pleasuring into intercourse. You can use any signal system you want, verbal or nonverbal, as long as your partner clearly receives and understands your communication. It's unrealistic to assume the man is always ready and willing to have sex – this expectation can create undue pressure.

The optimal relationship is one in which both partners feel comfortable initiating intercourse and both feel they have the right to say 'no'. If either partner does not desire intercourse, he or she can suggest an alternative way to connect, like holding each other and talking or manually or orally stimulating each other to orgasm. If you do not desire intercourse, suggest an alternative sensual or erotic experience.

There's nothing 'wrong' with arousal not culminating in intercourse or orgasm. Sexual expression is a choice, not a duty.

Be sure to discuss your experience in the morning, focusing on how comfortable and clear your communication system was. If there was a problem, what would you be willing to try next time to improve the communication process and sexual experience? Sexual desire is enhanced by positive anticipation, choice, freedom, and open communication. Desire is subverted by pressure, performance demands, predictability, and viewing sex as a way to prove something to your partner. Openly communicating a range of alternative ways to stay connected facilitates a positive sexual experience, even if it does not include intercourse.

5) Expectancies

The goals here are:

• to negotiate using a style where each feels heard, respected and considered, instead of attempts to control or use power that make the loser want to withdraw emotionally or get even.

• to negotiate a relationship you both can live with joyfully.

Sustaining a pleasurable intimate relationship does not work by magic. It depends upon a set of skills and understandings which can be learned.

You have learned most of what you know about intimate relationships through your early experiences in your family. Your personal history has a great deal of influence on what happens in your current relationships – on your behavior, your feelings, your expectations. You can change these influences if you become aware of them and want to change. It is well worthwhile to sort through what you inherited, keeping what fits for today and changing what does not.

Your goal should be a relationship that both partners can live with joyfully. For this to happen, each partner must become able to identify his or her own feelings and needs, and learn to communicate them in such a way that they can get met. This means communicating one's needs and desires without making the other partner feel resentful, smothered, burdened, manipulated, or inadequate. It is possible to change your behavior, attitudes, and feelings in ways that contribute to this goal.

We can help you to make your wanted changes.

Establishing Questions

Part One

Does your bond with your partner satisfy your need for connecting?

Yes ___ No ___

Do you feel love, warm affection or passion when thinking of your partner?

Yes ___ No ___

Do you feel you are significant to your partner in some important way?

Yes ___ No ___

Do you feel your partner admires you in some aspects?

Yes ___ No ___

Do you feel you are able to get over hurt feelings associated with your partner, most of the time?

Yes ___ No ___

Can you see your marriage moving forward in a positive sense?

Yes ___ No ___

Do you feel your partner respects you enough in your marriage?

Yes ___ No ___

Do you trust your partner?

Yes ___ No ___

Do you feel your partner listens to you, is hearing your messages, most of the time?

Yes ___ No ___

Do you feel communication about difficult topics between you and your partner is adequate?

Yes ___ No ___

For the above questions, each 'Yes' answer = 1 point. ( )

Each 'No' answer is zero points. (0)

Total score = _____

Part Two

Do you feel abandoned by your partner?

Yes ___ No ___

Do you feel in some way used or abused by your partner?

Yes ___ No ___

Do you feel in some way denied as a person by your partner?

Yes ___ No ___

Do you feel rejected by your partner?

Yes ___ No ___

Do you fear or dislike your partner's opinion or judgments of you in some way?

Yes ___ No ___

Do you fear your partner in any way?

Yes ___ No ___

Do you feel your partner is cheating on you?

Yes ___ No ___

Do you feel associated emotions (anger, jealousy, sadness, hurt)?

Yes ___ No ___

Do you feel your partner's behavior or needs are unpredictable?

Yes ___ No ___

Do you feel criticized a lot by your partner?

Yes ___ No ___

Do you feel your partner does not allow you sufficiently to be who you are?

Yes ___ No ___

For the above questions, each 'Yes' answer = zero points (0)

Each 'No' answer = 1 point (_)

Total score = _____

Final Score is the total number of points for both parts.

Part One = ____

Part Two = ____

Final score = ____

If your final score is 0 to 5 points:

You have an obvious marriage problem in which essentials are lacking. This final score is a poor result, indicating that your marriage at this moment is poor in trust, respect or affection. You experience quite a lot of criticism from your spouse or denial of who you really are. Maybe you feel rejected by your spouse or not totally accepted. This result indicates that some essential work is needed to get this marriage moving forward positively. For now, appreciate your courage to face the true state your marriage is in and ask yourself this: Can I allow some hope that my marriage can improve?

Yes ___ No ___

If your final score is 6 to 10 points:

A lot has probably happened, but some good feeling is still there. Your marriage is not in a good shape at this moment. The basics of the relationship – trust, affection, respect, communication – are lacking. A lot of things may have happened between you and your spouse, but some positive or warm feeling may still be present. You may want to hang on to these feelings and from there, start taking steps to improve your marriage. Think this over: Do you believe you can work things out to take your marriage to a higher level (more trusting, respecting and affectionate)?   Yes ___ No ___

If your final score is 11 to 15 points:

This is a good score, so let's bring your marriage to an even higher level! There are some points in your marriage that could be better, but a good and strong basis is present in your relationship. Certain areas can be improved to make your marriage really a dream marriage!

Think this over:

What can you do to bring your marriage to a higher level?

_____

_____

If your final score is 16 to 20 points:

You have a wonderful marriage. There is enough affection, love, respect, communication and no hard feelings. You feel you have a strong bond which gives you exactly what you emotionally need. Your marriage can take on a lot of challenges. Appreciate and celebrate having this wonderful marriage, as it is truly magnificent to have a marriage where both you and your spouse can be who you really are, have a strong and loving bond and grow individually while being together. Express it! Celebrate it!

In Closing

In our Dynamic Discovery workshops, the Leader poses a statement, then asks the group two questions. These two questions are very similar to what has been asked before: You go to sleep tonight and a miracle happens. All the advances in your life and your community that you hoped to happen have taken place. The miracle happens while you are asleep so you don't actually know that it has happened. When you wake up in the morning, what is the first thing that you will notice you are doing that will tell you the miracle has happened?

_____

_____

What next?

_____

_____

_____

See if you can place yourself into the 'questions' above, bearing in mind that problems are often defined in terms of what others do – situations that you might not feel you have influence over. That is why your emphasis must be on what will be different about yourself – because you do have the power to change that. Having a clear vision of what will be different, and that you know you have the power to change, is a significant step towards actually bringing it about.

By making the questions as open as possible, it is much more likely that the answers that come out of an actual workshop will be grounded in the group members' own experiences, yet will encompass endless possibilities. Notice that the questions are specifically not about changed circumstances due to some magic, but what you (and the other participants, if any) would be doing differently.

We tend to think of problems/difficulties as being ahead of us, and forget about the problems that have already been solved by our efforts.

In an actual workshop, we stay with the questions even if a client was to describe an 'impossible' solution, such as a deceased person being alive, and we acknowledge that wish and then ask, "How would that make a difference in your life?" Then as the client describes that he/she might feel as if they had their companion back again, we ask, "How would that make a difference?"

With that, the client might say something like, "I would have someone to confide in and support me." From there, we would ask the client to think of others in their life who could begin to be a confidante in a very small manner.

Rebuilding Your Marriage

If you are struggling with the concept of change, these questions catapult you from a problem-saturated context into a visionary context where you have a moment of freedom so as to step out of your problem story and into a story where you are more problem-free. But more importantly, it helps you identify exactly what you really want.

Even if it is only a question of surviving thus far, that alone is evidence of personal strengths and skills, which you can mobilize in the future.

Please remember this: Your mind is capable of performing many powerful tasks, and the most powerful is its ability to create concepts, because concepts become perceptions and – to your mind – perception is reality. In many instances, if your mind can conceive it, your mind and body can achieve it.

From concept to perception to achievement only requires that you take action … after you've made a plan and established the resources necessary to at least allow you to start. Once you've started on a path you really want to follow, you will always find a way to get whatever you need to continue on.

At the risk of sounding 'airy-fairy', I can highly recommend the following: Do whatever it takes to develop an 'attitude of gratitude'. The more you recognize and express gratitude for the things you have, the more things you will have to express gratitude for.

Without gratitude, happiness is rare. With gratitude, the odds for happiness go up dramatically. Giving thanks brings joy. You and I can find all kinds of things for which we can give thanks.

If you have questions or concerns, please contact us through our website, we also have several other free resources available. www.DynamicDiscovery.ca

Resources

Credit for much of my base of knowledge belongs to:

* The Alandel School and Clinic (hypnotherapy training).

* 20 years' experience working as a counselor and employee assistance program manager for Human Resources Services Ltd. (HRS).

* The Heartview Foundation of Mandan, North Dakota, where I learned about addictions.

* 26 years of immersion in the program of Alcoholics Anonymous.

* 25 years of studying various programs/approaches such as NLP, Psychology, Cognitive Behavioural Therapy, Quantum Physics and Reality Therapy

* Abraham Maslow's hierarchy of needs.

* Dr. William Glasser, who developed Reality Therapy / Control Theory.

* The writings of Milton Erickson which drew upon his own experiences to provide examples of the power of the unconscious mind. He was largely self-taught.

* Dave Elman, who was self-taught and wrote "Hypnotherapy" which was self-published.

* The book Alcoholics Anonymous (commonly known as The Big Book), the members I've come to know and love both in AA and its sister organization, Alanon.

* The teachings of Socrates, especially those concerning inductive reasoning (to draw logical conclusions) and his Four Basic Principles of Philosophy

* The writings of Napoleon Hill, who enjoyed a long and successful career writing, teaching, lecturing about the principles of success, and whose work is still relevant for those seeking personal achievement and motivation.

* The writings of Carlos Castaneda – particularly The Teachings of Don Juan – who was an American author with a Ph.D. in anthropology

* Tony Robbins - The Six Human Needs.

* Manfred Max-Neef (along with Antonio Elizalde and Martin Hopenhayn) developed the theory of Human Needs and Human-Scale Development.

Personal

Prior to developing the DYNAMIC DISCOVERY process I was presenting and leading a two day seminar program - I called *"THE PERSONAL IMPROVEMENT SERIES"* - that consisted of 4 topics, each of which were 4 hours in duration, typically presented on Saturday and Sunday. The 4 topics were: Intimate Relationships; Guilt; dependency, and; The Right To Choose.

I worked with several groups of clients from whom I learned some things that were never on my agenda. I did not want to be a counselor or therapist, and I certainly did not want to be anyone's advisor; I just enjoyed presenting information to people who were interested in looking at ways to make changes in their lives. Those first clients lead me into this process of self-evaluation through their enthusiastic and active participation which turned my seminars (or workshops) into participatory group sessions.

Because this is a <u>self-evaluation</u> process there are no experts or gurus; all I know that my clients don't know is the progression of the process and what the next question will be.

I am sincerely grateful to all those early clients who taught me so much.

George Bissett

Sample from Blaming

Don't just do something, find someone to blame!

I got to wondering if there was a service that I could offer that would be extremely valuable to humankind and – because of all the blaming going on – made my decision. So, I put my big brain to work and came up with a few pages of helpful material and – best of all – a really catchy jingle:

When your life is up in flames

and you don't know who to blame,

who you gonna call?

Blame Busters!

Blame Busters!

Blame Busters!

When your life is full of pain

and you got no one to blame,

who you gonna call?

Blame Busters!

Blame Busters!

Blame Busters!

And then you can repeat the last line several times… if you wish.

Come on, admit it; it's a catchy jingle and you'll be singin' and hummin' it all the time. Of course, this brilliant jingle won't really fix anything, but it is a nice diversion. You're welcome.

The Beginning

So, as I said, the idea for this piece on blame came upon me because I became overwhelmingly aware of all the blame that is all around us. Although it's not something we're born with, it is something we learn very early on.

For instance…

Picture a young boy or girl all alone in the living room and a parent enters only to see the spreading stain from a spilled glass of milk or juice. "What happened here?" the parent asks. With a shrug, the child answers, "I don't know. Don't blame me."

And then that child grows up and becomes a defense attorney who becomes skilled at conveying to their clients – ranging from rambunctious teens to criminal masterminds – that avoiding blame by shifting it to other people, places and things is their ticket to freedom.

"He (or they) did it, not me. Blame them, not me." "I'm a victim of the mean streets I live on. Don't blame me." "The cops planted (that evidence) on me. Blame them, not me." "It was the Twinkies. Blame the Twinkie-makers, not me." "I bin framed. I bin bamboozled. I'm not to blame."

Or, that child becomes a politician and lands in the middle of a scandal. When interviewed, the lament goes something like this:

"I'm just a politician. Blame the civil servants for the lost millions, not me"... because politicians only accept credit, never blame."

Or, that child becomes an adult, marries, gets caught in an adulterous situation and attempts to deflect responsibility by saying something like:

"If you had paid me more attention I wouldn't have had to..." or "He (or she) badgered me until they wore me down and I just couldn't resist any more." Or, the best one of all: "I don't know how it happened... it just did."

And so on. And to what end?

Nothing positive. Blaming resolves nothing. Blaming never prevents reoccurrence. Blaming is meant to harm others. It is referred to as the "Throw them under the bus" defense.

Has the foregoing made you feel sad? Now would be a good time to sing my jingle. Very loud. And repetitively.

If the 'blame card' doesn't work, we often move right into anger.

Anger

Humans have a wide range of emotions, and anger is a perfectly acceptable and common one. We all feel the need to address our frustrations, and to take quick action to alleviate our anger. But when do you know that anger is beyond your control and that you might have an anger management issue on your hands?

Go to our website, www.DynamicDiscovery.ca to find out the warning signs, and what you can do about it. Also, if you're a parent, learn how to discern between clumsy and aggressive behavior in your child, and how you can deal with your child's temper tantrums.

Or, you could just sing my jingle. Loudly. Repetitively.

Everyone gets mad at some time or another. But what if all you could think about was 100 ways to get even with that "so and so who did such and such to you"? That could be a signal that anger is affecting your life more than you think. Learn about other warning signs and ways to help deal with your anger and rage.

Let's face it…

Everyone gets angry.

Even "saints-in-training" get irked by some events that trigger an upsetting or aggressive response. Most of us will get over it; time will pass, the world goes on, and tomorrow will be another day. But for others, anger can build up over time and has the potential of reaching a dangerous and serious point.

Like any emotion, anger is normal. It helps the individual in dealing with a tense or troubling situation by offering an outlet of release. By the same token, however, too much of it bottled inside at the same time, or blowing too much steam all at once, can turn anger from a healthy life management tool into an ugly problem that hurts you and those around you.

While anger is normal, there are some symptoms that you should watch out for that may indicate that it is a life-interfering problem.

- You may have to address your anger if you can't get it off your mind and it consumes you and spills over into other things. Maybe you can't meet an obligation at home or work because all you can think about is how someone in your life was such a self-centered, inconsiderate jerk. Or all you talk about to your best friend is how much you hate that jerk, and all that complaining is ruining your nights as well as your days.

- Anger could be serious if it was caused by something that happened quite a while ago and you can't let go of it.
- If your anger results in plotting to carry out vengeful plans to hurt others you are working against your Best Interest: which is when you focus on hurting others instead of helping yourself. This is serious and extremely immature behavior.

Too much, or inappropriate, anger can be detrimental to your physical and mental health. In terms of physiology, it can result in ulcers and heart disease. And with emotional well-being, it could affect your relationships with those around you, your career, and other important institutions in your life. But there are some strategies you can employ to help identify and resolve your anger during the actual moment, and some long-term guidelines that can assist you in approaching life from a calmer perspective.

When anger happens, admit that you are angry, and release it - to an extent. Think moderation, and don't keep it bottled inside. Avoid overreaction by taking a step back.

Remove yourself from the situation and ask yourself if someone else in your place would be reacting in the same manner. Look at the situation, too; is it really that bad that it's worth getting all worked up about?

Try to think about something else when you feel that rush of anger. Hum a favorite song (or a perky jingle) or recall a happy moment instead of giving Tailgating-Tom the one-fingered salute via your rear view mirror.

Identify the source of your anger, and try to deal with him or her directly in a peaceful and productive manner. Also listen carefully to what others have to say, and wait until they're finished before you speak. It's amazing how words get misconstrued just by jumping in too soon. Allowing the few extra moments for the other person to finish also gives you time to absorb what is being said and formulate an appropriate response.

There are a number of actions you can take to help channel your anger from an unpredictable and volatile problem into a controlled response framed by a new, more relaxed attitude. For instance, avoid blaming yourself, even if you feel that it is your mistake and your mistake alone. Make the best of a bad situation and learn from the experience instead, especially if it's a situation beyond your control, such as a job lay-off. Check out how other people have handled the same problem and determine what coping mechanisms they used.

Help release your anger and any residual tension by discovering outlets. Physical activities are a great way to blow off steam in a positive way and give you time to calm down and assess your situation. Find other outlets, such as boxercise, weight workouts, jogging, walking, tai chi, yoga, keeping a journal, relaxation therapy, meditation and deep-breathing exercises. Get in touch with your funny bone and learn to laugh at yourself. Not everything has to be three-piece-suited serious. Laugh and loosen that necktie a bit… maybe a whole lot.

If you like what you have read please scan this code to buy it through Amazon

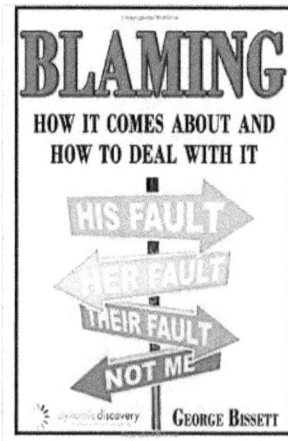

www.ingramcontent.com/pod-product-compliance
Lightning Source LLC
Chambersburg PA
CBHW070523030426
42337CB00016B/2073